THE THIRD REFORMATION IS COMING

How God will Radically Redefine the Church Today

Scott Wallis

Lighthouse Publications

The Third Reformation is Coming
by Scott Wallis

Printed in the United States of America
ISBN 0-9642211-4-4

Unless otherwise indicated, Bible quotations are taken from the King James Version.

Publisher
Lighthouse Publications
2028 Larkin Avenue
Elgin, IL 60123
(847) 468-1457
www.ScottWallis.org

Author
Scott Wallis
www.ScottWallis.org

Cover Design
Scott Wallis & Associates
2028 Larkin Avenue
Elgin, IL 60123
(847) 468-1457

Foreword

by Apostle Burton W. Seavey

• The Third Reformation is Coming •

Should you be reading this Foreword to gain a glimpse of the author's intent in writing this book, don't allow the term *Reformation* to frighten you away. It almost scared me away, also – until I had the pleasure of reading the entire manuscript, and understood the reason why that word, *Reformation*, was chosen. As you read, you will understand that this book isn't merely another *They Ought to Do Things My Way*, book, but rather, a clarion call to the Church to wake up to its inner potentials as revealed in Scripture.

As I read further, I heard the heart of the Holy Spirit to unite God's people as never before – to draw us together with bonds of His holy love. One great problem within the Church today is the pitifully few believers who have left the milk of the Word and progressed on to the meat, thereby growing up in Christ.

In my more than forty-five years of ministry, I have never read (even in my own book, *Shock Wave*) or heard a more concise call for unity in the body of Christ, than in this book. Satan has hypnotized the people of God into believing that a "One Church" mentality will lead to the anti-Christ.

The fact is that denominationalism is one of Satan's greatest tools. Every time a new "schism" arises, a new "name" is affixed to it, and we have just witnessed the birth of a new denomination. The moment we hear the name of the denomination to which someone belongs, we immediately know what he/she believes – and WHERE WE DISAGREE!!! In other words, when we form a denomination around a set of doctrines, instead of around Jesus, He ceases to be the center of thought and focus. We then surround the doctrine with great, high walls to protect it from "outsiders." In short, the "doctrine" often supplants the place and privilege that belongs solely to Jesus Christ, and often assures that there will now be division between followers of various denominations. Allow me to quote Pastor Wallis's own words from chapter two: *"Here we define a reformational movement as a fundamental transformation in believer's understanding of Christ, such that, **it completely changes the form and function of the Church**"* (emphasis mine).

Most of Christendom believes, in one form or another, that Jesus is coming soon. (Immediately, I've opened up at least three, perhaps four different views as to precisely when Jesus will return in relation to the Great Tribulation: pre-trib, mid-trib, post-trib!) For now, let's lay aside all that and agree on "pan-trib" – i.e., it'll all "pan out" in the end! The Holy Spirit is endeavoring to bring many sons to maturity, and that maturity, of necessity, means that we will ban together as a mighty army against the archenemy of the Church: Satan.

Satan does not fear your denomination, by whatever title it may hail. The only thing Satan fears is when the people of God lay down their divisions and solidify themselves in the unity of the faith – the fundamental faith in Jesus Christ! Pastor Wallis wrote, *"God has called us to be a glorious Church ... designed to displace the current divisions among churches, leaders and believers, so that we can become a united Body of Christ under the leadership of the Holy Spirit."* Then, he goes on to say, *"We are moving from the mentality that has promoted the mindset of the individualistic priesthood of believers into an understanding of God **that focuses our attention upon our role as a Kingdom of priests"*** (emphasis mine).

This is, beyond any shadow of a doubt, the Church's finest hour. The Holy Spirit is calling you to find your way into the Holy of Holies, where you will come face-to-face with the Lord Jesus Christ. He's calling us to "Come away with Me, My beloved," as He enfolds us in His arms of love. The Lord Jesus is calling, wooing His Bride to steal away from the maddening crowds, from the TV set or whatever commands your greatest attention. He is asking you to simply focus that same attention on Him! Quality time spent away with Him will reward you with spiritual understandings and guidance for your life and ministry. But beyond all that, as wonderful as it is, you'll find yourself not alone in the Holy of Holies. What you'll find will be a multitude of people, who like yourself, have laid aside doctrinal differences to enter the Holy of Holies, focusing not on doctrine, but on the One by Whom we are all named – JESUS!

Apostle Burton W. Seavey
Osceola, Indiana

• The Third Reformation is Coming •

Contents

Introduction

Behold, how good and pleasant it is for brethren to dwell together in unity! It is like the precious ointment upon the head, that ran down upon the beard, even Aaron's beard: that went to the skirts of his garments; as the dew that descended upon the mountains of Zion: for there the Lord commanded the blessing, even life forevermore.

Ps. 133:1-3

Unity is one of the most powerful forces in the universe. God has commanded a blessing upon those who choose to dwell in this place called unity. The very spring of heaven's life opens to us when we choose by an act of our will to lay aside our own agenda and lose ourselves in the purpose and plan of God.

The Bible itself reveals a day in which all things will be drawn into the very center of God's will. God is moving everything in all of creation toward this appointed place in time. Paul in writing about this specific day says this, *"That in the dispensation of the fullness of times He might gather together in one all things in Christ, both things which are in heaven, and things which are on earth; even in him..."* (Eph. 1:10).

My heart yearns for this day when all things are subdued to the purpose and plan of God as revealed through the person of Jesus Christ. Much of my life has been devoted to the passionate pursuit of the presence of Christ. This has been my singular pursuit since becoming a Christian in 1987. I have personally spent untold hours in prayer pursuing God – and still long for more. I want more of Him in my life.

Over the years, as I have walked with Christ in that secret place of prayer, something has become evident to me regarding the reception of the fullness of God's presence: I alone cannot receive all that God has for me. The fullness of God can only be accessed in the midst of believers united in their quest for more of God's presence. The Church is designed to function properly where believers are completely dependent upon one another. The Church cannot be the Church until, and unless, we are willing to become dependent upon one another.

We are One in the Spirit

Understanding this dependence between believers is the underlying revelation contained within this book. My desire is to reveal to the Church one of the greatest gifts ever given to us by God – the Unity of the Spirit. This gift has laid dormant and gone unnoticed for centuries. Most believers are unaware of its existence. And few know how to tap into the unique power afforded to us by God through it.

The Church is designed for greatness. God has deposited something great inside of His Church – Himself. And yet this deposit can only be withdrawn by a group of believers who are united with God and one another in purpose and destiny. Those willing to connect with other believers in a common goal and in the process lose their identity so that they might find their true identity in Christ alone.

This should be the motto of the Church – Christ Alone. Those who have made this their motto have seen tremendous power displayed by the awesome hand of God. God's hand can only be unveiled in a place where people are in one accord. In other words, before the Holy Spirit could move in power, as He desired on the day of Pentecost, believers needed to be in one accord. The Holy Spirit was waiting for unity then and He is still waiting for unity today. True unity is what the Holy Spirit is looking for so that He can openly display His power on behalf of those who believe in Christ's name. The Holy Spirit is looking for churches and believers who have discovered the secret – we are already one – and have chosen to walk in this spirit of unity by faith.

The Church is already one Body. God has never divided His Church into many different bodies. There is only one Body, one faith and one Lord who is above all and through all and in us all. We have all been united together by the same Spirit who dwells within us. This is the reality of the Body of Christ – we are one Body. Understanding this reality is the key to walking in the supernatural dimension of the corporate man revealed in the Scriptures.

The Corporate Man

The Church today knows little of the corporate man revealed in scripture instead we have mostly been spoon-fed Pabulum. True maturity is not how much I alone can accomplish for God in my life. No matter how noble what I do for God's kingdom may appear to be, it can never compare to what the corporate man can accomplish. Real faith is not and has never been individualistic in nature.

No, real faith has a corporate mindset where it views how its actions affect the entire Body. This is the reality of the kingdom – my actions do affect those around me. What I do or don't do can help or hinder the growth of Christ's Body. Both sins of omission and commission are serious in the sight of God. This is why it is essential for the Church to learn how important the corporate man is in the sight of God.

How important is the corporate man in the sight of God? I will use an illustration given by Christ Himself.

Jesus said, *"If thy right eye offend thee, pluck it out, and cast it from thee: for it is profitable for thee that one of thy members should perish, and not that thy whole body should be cast into hell. And if thy right hand offend thee cut it off, and cast it from thee: for it is profitable for thee that one of thy members should perish, and not that thy whole body should be cast into hell"* (Matt. 5:29-30).

Was Jesus simply talking about a man lusting in his heart after a woman such that he commits adultery with her in his heart? Or could it be that Jesus was seeking to reveal to His Church a principle showing the importance of unity in the Body of Christ? I will leave that question for you to answer. I already know what I believe. I am persuaded that Christ was talking about much more than a man committing adultery in his heart in this passage of scripture. I believe that Jesus was seeking to convey to us the reality of the corporate man revealed in scripture.

My hope is that as we move forward you will begin to understand and see clearly what I am seeking to convey in this book regarding God's great gift of unity to the Church – we are one. I am doing this so that the Church today can begin to unite as the corporate man revealed in scripture. Without this simple yet profound revelation, I believe that the Church will continue to wallow in the same strife and division that has brought us to a barren and fruitless place of busyness and activity rather than the kingdom of God, which is righteousness, peace and joy in the Holy Spirit.

As such, I pray that God *"may give unto you the spirit of wisdom and revelation in the knowledge of Him: the eyes of your understanding being enlightened that ye may know what is the hope of His calling, and what the riches of the glory of His inheritance in the saints, and what is the exceeding greatness of his power to us-ward who believe, according to the working of His mighty power..."* (Eph. 1:18).

Chapter One

The Clarion Call of Christ

For ye are yet carnal: for whereas there is among you envying, and strife, and divisions, are ye not carnal, and walk as men?

1 Cor. 3:3

*A*re ye not carnal? Paul asked the church at Corinth. Here was their spiritual father giving them the whipping of their life, and they knew it. This question cut straight to the heart of their spiritual condition. With one word, he located them and brought them to the realization of their dire spiritual state. This was not what they expected. They expected Paul to throw his arms around them and say, "I love you." Instead Paul chose to say "I love you" with his rod of correction. He disciplined them because he knew where they were heading. Paul knew that a little leaven would eventually leaven the whole lump. Paul knew that unless he acted

9

quickly that his baby church would mutate and turn into a spiritual mega-monster. This is what he wanted to avoid at all costs. This is why Paul took such drastic measures he wanted to root out this little leaven before it had time to fill the whole church – and he did.

What was the leaven that Paul was so terrified of as the spiritual father of this baby Corinthian church? Division. Paul was terrified that division had crept into the Corinthian church and would spread through it. This left a bad taste in Paul's mouth and Paul knew what it was – flesh. The carnality of the Corinthian church was coming out. Their desire to promote themselves, their agendas and those they followed came out; they were glorying in men. They were more concerned with the things of men than the things of God. And in the same way that Christ rebuked Peter for this, so now Paul also was rebuking the Corinthian church. This was not a minor spiritual transgression, as it would seem to many of us. No, it was a major spiritual flaw and Paul knew it. This is why he rebuked them for it. And what a stinging rebuke it was. They were rebuked for being unspiritual carnal fleshly creatures; they were acting just like newborn babies in Christ. And Paul was telling them in no uncertain terms: stop being babies and grow up!

This could not have been a more humbling word for them to receive. Not only did they have to receive this message, but they also had to swallow it. A good friend of mine once sent me a fax with a message on it saying, "be careful what you say for tomorrow you may have to eat your words." And this is exactly what the Corinthian church had to do. They had to swallow their pride and eat their words along with a large portion of humble pie. God humbled them because their knowledge, eloquence and giftedness had puffed them up. Pride was the source of their division. Not the normal natural pride found in the unregenerate man, but rather a more hideous form of pride – spiritual pride.

Spiritual Pride and Impending Disaster

Believers in the church at Corinth had become the spiritual know-it-alls of their day – the "Bible Answer Men and Women" of the New Testament. They thought that they knew all there was to know about God. They thought they had God figured out. After all, Paul was their spiritual father. Apollos was their pastor and teacher. They had it made. God was moving in their midst. Gifts were being manifested. The five-fold ministry was well established. Believers were even seeing open visions of angels. When they came together, everyone had something to share about what God was doing in their life or speaking to them. They were a church on fire for God or so it would seem.

In reality, from God's perspective they were as babies before Him, not because of the experiences they had, but because of the unity they lacked. Their division was a major blemish upon their spiritual condition – a blemish that was like a giant pimple on the face of this church in the sight of God. This was not a pretty sight to God. In fact, the great Physician, Christ Jesus, saw this growth not as a mild teenage blemish but as a potential cancer that could destroy the spiritual state of his entire body.

I hope that you are seeing the picture that I am trying to paint with words of the spiritual condition of the church in Corinth. I am trying to convey the seriousness of their situation. I want you to understand how God saw all their envying, strife and division from His perspective. Please listen closely to the words that I am sharing right now from my heart.

The church at Corinth was in bad shape; they were being wounded by one another. Their hearts were calloused by their own condition. They could not recognize the iceberg that lay ahead directly in front of their path if they did not change their course. They were on a collision course with disaster and they didn't know it. Like the passengers on the titanic, they were oblivious to the potential danger that lay ahead.

And yet, in spite of all these potential dangers that could capsize them at any moment they still had a ship – a unified church – with which to ride through the storms of life. They had an ark of safety that was still intact, even though in some cases, it was being held together by gum and glue. They were still safe from the storms of life and strategies of Satan, though it was only by the mercy of Almighty God. And they were carnal? What then are we?

Pride in the Church Today

I cannot even imagine what God must see day after day when He looks down from heaven at His Church in our day. We are in worse condition than the Corinthian church ever was. We are worse spiritually in that we don't have the tremendous gifts, as a whole, that they did. Our pride and arrogance is much greater than theirs even though we have less knowledge than they did. Our moral condition is worse in that we don't, won't or can't even correct those who are in blatant sin. And as far as leadership goes, how can we ever even think that our present leadership could compare to the likes of Paul, Apollos and Peter. Most importantly, in spite of all their bickering and backbiting, there was only one church in Corinth, not hundreds or thousands.

Beloved, we are well behind the Corinthian church in every way. When we look at them we should marvel at where they were at and hope that we could get there. Instead, we say of them that they were the unspiritual ones of the Early Church. In reality, this group of believers whom Paul called carnal was more spiritual than us on our best days. They knew more about God, had more of God, and went further for God than any church group or movement that has been around for the past 1,800 years. I hope that you are beginning to catch a glimpse at the state of the modern Church.

Church, We Have a Problem

The Church today consists of several thousand denominations not just churches. We call ourselves everything from Baptist to Pentecostal to Charismatic to Evangelical to Catholic. We are a divided Church – and we think it is O.K. We are satisfied with the sad state that we are in at the present time. We do not even want to imagine that there is only one Church – this thought terrifies us. To some this idea even sounds cultic or devilish. Some have even used this sign of unity as a mark of the beast, a sign of the coming anti-Christ. We are deceived and we don't even know it. We have believed a lie and think that it is now the truth. We use terms like division is God's tool of multiplication in the kingdom. We call our denomination or network our own tribe, family and covering. And these smooth words sound oh, so good, but they are laced with error.

We are living a lie and don't even realize it. We are carnal and think that we are being spiritual. We have introduced error upon error that has fed the need to appease our consciences from the guilt we feel over being a divided Church. And instead of calling it sin, we call it expedient and convenient – in other words, "That's just the way things are, so live with it." What we ought to be doing is falling on our faces and weeping over the sin of division we have tolerated in the Church for far too long. We need a real revival of repentance that will bring real unity in the Church today. Anything less is, at best, a token of God's mercy and, at worst, a sign of God's impending judgment. Precious saint of God, my question to you is: Are we not carnal?

I hope that this chapter has pricked your heart. My desire is to provoke you into genuine heartfelt repentance over our present state. I am in just as bad of shape as you. I am not pointing the finger at you, but at myself and every other leader who has divided in the name of Christ. We are guilty before a holy God. We desperately need His mercy, for we don't know how to get out of the mess that we have made of things. It was so easy when God gave birth to it. The Church was His beautiful baby, His prized possession. How is it that we have mutated into a monster? How is it that we have become the enemy of God?

God, not the devil, is the primary one fighting against us. He is shaking us in hopes that we will wake up out of the state of division that we have fallen into. God is confronting our error in hopes of bringing us to repentance so that He might heal us. It is His desire to heal us, to work in and through us. But before this can happen He must unify us. My prayer is that God would truly do a work of repentance in you as you read the rest of this book to bring into your heart the same desire He has put in my heart for unity.

Chapter Two

• The Third Reformation is Coming •

The Third Day
Church is Coming

---

*After two days will He revive us: in the third
day He will raise us up, and we shall live in
His sight.*

Hos. 6:2

The Church today is in a state of transition and transformation. A metamorphosis has begun – we are moving from what has been into what will be. The Church of the future has begun today. God is doing something new in His Church. As such, many are asking these questions: "How will the new move of God look, and what do I need to do to be a part of it?"

Some have already started answering these questions. Dr. Bill Hamon has written an excellent book on ministering in the marketplace called, *The Day of the Saints*. I believe this book is the capstone to what we have known as the Pentecostal Movement. Another great book on the coming reformation within the Church is by author Sammy Rodriguez, called, *Are You a Third Day Christian?* This book identifies the reality of a coming third day movement and what it will mean to the Church.

I believe that the Church is entering a third day or a third reformational age. This Third Day Church can be identified in the prophecy given in Hosea 6:2. This verse specifically speaks to Christ's resurrection. Also, according to some scholars, it points to a third reformational move within the Church. (Scriptures can and often do have more than one meaning or application.)

New Paradigms of Understanding

Historically, with each reformational movement of the Holy Spirit there comes a corresponding change in the understanding of the Church. This paradigm shift in the understanding of the Church causes believers to view their relationship with Christ in completely new ways. Eyes and ears that were closed to what the Holy Spirit is saying, open, with an increased accuracy and revived sense of desire for the person of Christ.

The Holy Spirit draws us into deeper dimensions of what Christ has purchased for us through His death, burial and resurrection. In other words, renewed revelation creates a new frame of reference opening new doorways into the Holy Spirit's presence so believers can experience more of Christ. As believers experience more of Christ, the Church changes through the process of reformation/restoration.

Every reformational/restorational movement within the Church has followed the pattern set forth above. The Church over the past five hundred years has experience two different reformational movements and several smaller restorational movements. Here we define a reformational movement as a fundamental transformation in believers understanding of Christ, such that, it completely changes the form and function of the Church. From this definition of a reformational movement, we can further define a restorational movement as the process by which each reformational movement reaches full maturity and completion.

Three Reformational Movements

For the sake of time, I want to focus our attention upon the historical reformational movements, and the coming reformational movement.

The first reformational movement is known as the Protestant reformation. This reformational movement began when Luther nailed his *95 Theses* upon the doors of the Catholic church. This attempt at communication was interpreted as an attack upon the very foundations of the Catholic church. Luther's simple faith in the Word of God shot forth like a cannon demolishing traditional strongholds that were preventing people from receiving the free gift of salvation. Luther's revelation opened the way for everyone to be saved by grace through faith.

The second reformational movement, which began January 1, 1900, is called the Pentecostal reformation. (The reason that I am calling this the Pentecostal reformation and not the Pentecostal movement is simple: I believe that the Pentecostal movement is coming to full completion). The Pentecostal movement began as a group of Bible college students in Topeka, Kansas started seeking more of God through a deeper revelation of the Bible. In January 1900, the answer came. Agnes Osman received the free gift of the Holy Spirit with the corresponding sign of speaking in unknown tongues. (It was later verified by linguists that what she had written was actually a specific dialect of the Chinese language). For three days she was unable to speak or write in any other language than tongues. This supernatural sign signified the coming of the Pentecostal reformation.

Along with each of these first two reformational movements, there have been several restorational movements. Some of these restorational movements have included the following: the Moravian Revival, the Anabaptist Movement, the Holiness Movement, the Great Awakening, the Cane-Ridge Revival, the Welch Revival, the Healing Revival, the Jesus Movement, and the Charismatic Renewal. More recently, the Church has experienced several mini-revivals, including the Toronto Blessing, the Brownsville Revival and the Smithton

Outpouring. All of these restorational movements correspond to one of these two reformational movements.

This brings us to today and the present move of God – the third reformational movement. If there is a coming third reformational movement, as most leaders on the cutting edge of what the Holy Spirit is saying believe there is, then how will it look? How and when will we know it has come? And, what signs or experiences will be associated with it? Answering these and other similar questions will be critical in understanding the coming reformational movement and any restorational moves that may follow.

Three Corresponding Events

In order for us to look forward and identify what the coming third reformational movement will look like, and any signs that will be associated with it, I believe that we must first look backward, from a big picture perspective, and identify the significant events that occurred in each of the first two reformational movements. From my study of these first two reformational movements, I believe that there are at least three corresponding events that took place. These three significant events that took place in each of these reformational movements, thus altering the belief structure of the church, are as follows:

- A free gift was received
- A baptism was experienced
- A Levitical feast was observed

The first reformational movement revealed the free gift of salvation. This gift once received opened the door for the second experience of baptism, which was revealed during the Anabaptist movement. Romans 6:4 says, *"...we are buried with Him (Christ) by baptism into death: that like as Christ was raised up from the dead by the glory of the Father, even so we also should walk in newness of life."* The Father, who is the one that initiated this experience, was revealing and enabling us to partake of all that Christ provided through His death, burial and resurrection. The first Levitical feast – the Feast of Passover – signifies this.

The second reformational movement revealed to us the free gift of the Holy Spirit. This gift opened the door for us to experience a second baptism, the baptism in the Holy Spirit. The initiator of this baptism is Jesus Christ, the Son of God. John 1:33-34 says, *"...He that sent me to baptize with water, the same said unto me, upon whom thou shalt see the Spirit decending and remaining on Him, the same is He which baptizeth with the Holy Ghost. And I saw, and bare record that this is the Son of God."* The baptism of the Holy Spirit was given to enable believers to become witnesses of Christ's resurrection by the supernatural demonstration of His power. The second Levitical feast – the Feast of Trumpets – signifies this.

Now I believe that we are ready to move forward and begin taking a look at the coming third reformational movement. The three historical guideposts lighting our way to what this third reformational movement will look like are a free gift, a baptism and a feast.

The Final Stage is Set

From my study of the scriptures, I believe that the free gift being offered to the Body of Christ right now is the gift of the unity of the Spirit, the baptism being offered is the baptism into Christ's Body and the feast being prepared for us is the Feast of Tabernacles. Each one of these experiential practices is in the process of being restored to the Church and will be restored prior to the coming of our Lord and Savior Jesus Christ.

The third reformational movement is coming! The Father is preparing the way for the soon return of His Son. In order for His Son to return, there must be a radical reformation on the scale of the first two reformational movements. In a very real sense, we are currently living in our own dark ages. Our present dark age is just as real as the one facing Luther in his day. We may not be buying indulgences, clinging to promises of purgatory or denying God's power as religious people did in Luther's day, but believers today are in just as much bondage to a religious system that isn't working.

God has designed the third reformation to change all of that. Through this third reformational movement, every believer receiving the free gift, being baptized in today's baptism and partaking of today's feast will begin fulfilling their position in Christ's Body. This will prepare the way for Christ to return for a spotless bride without spot, wrinkle or any such thing.

God has called us to be a glorious Church. The way is now being made for us to become the glorious Church spoken of in Ephesians 4. God is opening the door for a third reformational movement to take place. This third reformational movement is designed to displace the current divisions among churches, leaders and believers so that we can become a united Body of Christ under the leadership of the Holy Spirit. As leaders, believers and churches enter this third reformational movement of the Holy Spirit, there will come a radical paradigm shift in our understanding and experience of Christ. As such, God is in the process of bringing radical change into His Church. We are moving from the mentality that has promoted the mindset of the individualistic priesthood of believers into an understanding of God that focuses our attention upon our role as a Kingdom of priests. This is where the emphasis will be in the third day of the Church.

We are the Third Day Church. God is raising us up in this day to do things a totally new and different way. Those who participate in the Third Day Church will experience Christ as they have never experienced Him before. What a privilege it is to be living in this day – the third day of the Church. This is the day of the raising up of the Body of Christ as Hosea and Ezekiel have prophesied, the manifestation and demonstration of

Christ's kingdom, resurrection power and soon return to a hurting world. Even so, come, Lord Jesus. Amen.

Chapter Three

How I Discovered the Unity of the Spirit

...Endeavouring to keep the unity of the Spirit in the bond of peace.

Eph. 4:3

I n 1987, while studying Electrical Engineering at the University of Iowa, some fellow classmates who were part of a local campus group called the Navigators began to share with me the gospel of Christ. To be honest, this was the first time I had ever heard anyone share anything similar to what these individuals were sharing. At first, I did not know if they were part of a cult, or crazy, or genuine Christians. All that I did know is they asked me to begin reading the Bible (the Gospel of John) which I agreed to do.

Reading the Bible opened my eyes to things that I did not know existed. Seeing what Jesus did and the way that He did things made me like Him. I liked the Jesus about Whom I was reading in the gospel of John. I can still remember that third day of reading about Christ on February 23rd, around midnight. I was in real spiritual darkness and the light was beginning to shine into my heart. I can still hear the words that echoed in my mind that night: "You're a sinner."

A Free Gift

Hearing these words broke me. Living a relatively moral life made me think that I was a good person. Surely God, if there were a God, would approve of my life. Sadly, I was wrong. My heart was broken by the fact that I was a sinner, and in one instant my heart in total submission to Christ began to call out: "Lord Jesus, I ask you to come into my life."

In an instant I became a new creature. I felt my sins physically lift from me. I was born from above. God was now my Father. I was accepted in the beloved. Immediately, I began sharing my newfound life in Christ with those who had witnessed to me of the love of my Savior Jesus Christ. They were as excited as I was. Soon, I began to tell everyone I met of the Jesus Who had now become real to me. I became a radical Bible believing Christian who fell in love with Christ.

Today, after years of studying the scriptures, I can now describe in detail from a scriptural standpoint what happened the moment I accepted Christ as my Savior. Unwittingly, I had appropriated Christ's sacrifice for myself when I heard the words that I was a sinner, and my heart became broken. I had placed my faith in Christ and His redemptive work for my salvation. My sins were completely washed away by the blood of Christ. I had accepted Christ's sacrificial gift at Calvary, which brought me into right standing before God so that I might become his adopted covenant son.

In other words, I had received the free gift of salvation provided for me by Christ. This gift was unearned and something that I could not attain on my own. No amount of work would have made me good enough in the sight of God to be brought into a right standing with Him. The only way that I could receive this free gift of salvation was by placing my faith in the already completed work of Christ at Calvary.

A Second Free Gift

Soon after receiving this free gift of salvation I became aware of another free gift offered to all Christians called the baptism in the Holy Spirit. How I stumbled upon this second free gift was entirely by accident as my heart became enraptured for more and more of Christ. My salvation experience had made me extremely hungry for the things of God. I began reading my Bible all the time, attending a local church and spending long moments alone with God in the secret place of prayer.

The local church that I attended, an Assembly of God church located in Iowa City, was a small comfortable Bible believing church. I attended services there every week going to both the Sunday morning Bible class and the following worship service. While there, I received a magazine called the Pentecostal Evangel, which I looked forward to reading each week.

One day, approximately one month after receiving the gift of salvation, I went back to my dorm room after the church service and began reading the Pentecostal Evangel. While reading through it that Sunday evening, I noticed the following title at the very beginning of the pamphlet: "What We Believe." Immediately upon seeing these words, the thought popped into my head: "I should find out what they believe."

Curiously, I began to read through the statement of faith located on the inside. As I was reading this statement of faith, I came to a passage that said, "We believe the Holy Spirit is given to those who ask for Him." Upon hearing this in my heart, it occurred to me that it wouldn't hurt. So I asked for the Holy Spirit.

An Unexpected Blessing

Amazingly, as soon as I asked for the Holy Spirit, words began to fill my mouth as I started speaking out in this strange language. To be honest, I was totally unprepared for what was happening. I was experiencing the supernatural realm, and it freaked me out. I was so startled by this experience that when it first happened I jumped up off the couch and looked around to see what was happening. I had just received the second free gift offered by God – the baptism in the Holy Spirit.

Today, I can scripturally share with you what happened at this moment when I asked for the gift of the Holy Spirit. I can prove scripturally that this free gift of the Holy Spirit is available to every born-again believer. I have personally led others in receiving this free gift of the Holy Spirit. I have witnessed believers who, as I have laid my hands upon them, have received this free gift of the Holy Spirit.

Why am I sharing this with you? In order to help you understand what we are about to embark on as we move forward in this chapter. I have stated everything to this point to help you understand that Christ has given gifts and that there is a prescribed way in the scriptures to receive these gifts. The gift of salvation is available to every person on planet earth. Anyone can be born again if they will only believe. Every believer has the ability to receive the free gift of the Holy Spirit if they will only believe. God has already made these two free gifts available to everyone, if and only if they will receive them by faith.

Still Another Free Gift

Now that I have laid a solid foundation for what I am saying in this chapter, I want to share with you some good news about a free gift Christ has given to His Church. Much of the Church still does not know about this gift or even think it exists. This free gift has the potential to radically change the face of the Church today in much the same way and to the same extent as the baptism of the Holy Spirit did to the Church in the early 20th Century. This is how important I believe this gift is to the Church today.

I first learned about this free gift offered by Christ to His Church as I began attending a local church in my hometown of Elgin, Illinois. It was December of 1992 when I walked in through the doors of this church. There was something special here that I had never felt at any of the other churches that I had been to before. I truly felt at home and was keenly aware that God was doing something special here, yet I did not know what it was.

The changes in my life during this time were dramatic. Prior to attending this church, I was going through severe trials on every level of my life. Nothing I did seemed to work. My life could be exemplified by the words "broke, busted and disgusted." The successes I had were usually short-lived and came with much effort and a great price. Nothing was ever easy and I was suffering a great deal in my life. I was always hanging on the edge never knowing what would happen from day to day. Life was hard.

Gradually, as I began attending this church week after week, things became better. My circumstances, which were next to impossible, began to get better. I soon saw the love of God being ministered in tangible practical everyday ways. There was food on my table, money for my rent, and I was finding purpose for my life. And the amazing thing about everything that was happening in my life is this: the leadership of the church did very little on a practical level to help facilitate what began happening in my life.

I began to see something that I had never seen before, that God works in a place of genuine unity. There was a genuine unity in this church. People truly cared for one another, and the leadership of the church helped facilitate this unity. As a result, God began to work supernaturally in and through the lives of those present. I was healed of much of what had happened previously in my life without ever really receiving prayer for it. The spirit of prophecy upon my life increased dramatically to such a degree that I could describe intimate details about events in people's lives. God was at work in my life and I personally loved what He was doing and wanted more.

Unfortunately, the pastor of this church left after a few years. I was devastated. Soon my life went into a tailspin again. For the next three years I struggled, as I had the previous years prior to coming to this church. Everything was different – the anointing that had been there lifted and soon many of the people who made this church what it was left. However, I remained in hopes that God would tell me what I should do next. I didn't want to leave this church without having some other place to go, so I stayed there for another three long years as I waited for God to speak to me about what I should do.

In July of 1998, I left this church and went down to Texas from Illinois for a 5-month period. During this time, I began to see doors open to me to minister the word of God. Even though I had prophesied extensively for the past ten years, I had never really been allowed by pastors to share the word of God in their churches. This began to change as God opened doors of utterance to me.

The Unity of the Spirit

The church where I preached my very first message was Shiloh Community Church, pastored by Steve Carpenter (currently the Director of Mike Bickle's Forerunner School of Prayer). The first message I ever preached was a message entitled *Cultivating the Miraculous through the Unity of the Spirit*. In that message, I began to share about my experiences at the church I had attended previously and how God had moved so mightily in my life. Within the content of this message, I began to understand something powerful that I had never before seen in scripture – that there was a free gift of unity available to the Church.

Suddenly, I saw that many leaders' attempts at attaining unity were in vain because they were not done according to the pattern revealed in scripture. God has already made us, His Church, one and given us this unity as a free gift. This free gift of unity is called the unity of the Spirit and is available to every local church where the leaders and believers within that local church openly receive by faith this free gift of the unity of the Spirit.

Local churches that begin receiving this free gift of the unity of the Spirit begin to function differently than local churches who have not received this gift. Churches that have not received this gift will inevitably focus upon the individual needs of the people within the church and much of what happens in the church will be directed to believers individually. In other words, the message of this kind of church is that we are a priesthood of believers and we can individually receive what God has for us. In this instance, the local church exists for the people. On the other hand, churches that receive the free gift of the unity of the Spirit make their focus the needs of the Kingdom. Their message is that we are a Kingdom of priests unto God. In this instance, the local church exists to advance Christ's kingdom.

These are the differences we are facing in the days ahead as God moves His Church and people toward a kingdom mindset. We are becoming more and more a corporate man as the scriptures reveal. God is drawing everything into His Son. Christ is fast becoming all in all. This Church is the End-Time Church spoken of in scripture – a Church on fire with the power of the Holy

Spirit. And we are called to become members in this Church for the purpose of advancing Christ's kingdom.

In order for this to happen, we must understand and receive this free gift of the unity of the Spirit. We can only receive this free gift by a corporate faith, brought about through the leadership of the local church. The degree to which a local church walks in this free gift will often be the level of understanding a pastor or leader has of this free gift.

Apostolic Ministry

As the tongue of the church, pastors have the ability to direct the church where they believe it should go. In order for pastors to direct their church toward the unity of the Spirit, they must have a grasp of this unity from a scriptural standpoint. Moreover, they must have the practical means necessary to live it, apostolically. This is one of the main reasons why God is speaking so much of the apostolic ministry. It takes the mentorship of genuine apostles to lead the church into the corporate faith necessary to receive the free gift of the unity of the Spirit.

Genuine apostolic ministry will create an atmosphere for this unity of the Spirit to begin, and pastors through their loving care will help nurture believers so that they can walk in this place of unity on a daily basis. This is why apostles are so important to the Church and desperately needed today. Genuine apostles and true apostolic ministry create unity within the Church. In fact,

I am persuaded that this is one of the primary characteristics of genuine apostolic ministry.

In the next chapter, I will lay a solid scriptural foundation through various proof texts for this free gift of the unity of the Spirit and how Christ has paid the price for us to have it. After I have done this, I will then provide some practical methods to walk in this unity within the local church. To God be the Glory!

Chapter Four

Receiving the Free Gift of the Unity of The Spirit

As every man hath received the gift, even so minister the same one to another, as good stewards of the manifold grace of God.

1 Pet. 4:10

One of the things that the Church has yet to learn is how to receive the free gift of the unity of the Spirit. This gift is free in the same way that salvation and the baptism in the Holy Spirit are free. In the last chapter, I talked a little about my experience in receiving the free gift of salvation, the baptism in the Holy Spirit, and my understanding of the unity of the Spirit.

In this chapter, I want to offer a solid scriptural frame of reference for you to understand how God gave this free gift of the unity of the Spirit, how we can receive it, and how we are to keep it once we have it. To do this, I will lay an extensive foundation of scriptures, explaining what they mean and how they apply to us today. You may not have often heard many of the scriptures that I will use. As such, I will spend much of this chapter talking about how they relate to one another.

Our first scripture revealing that the unity of the Spirit is a gift can be found in Ephesians 4:3: *"Endeavoring to keep the unity of the Spirit in the bond of peace."* Although this verse does not clearly tell us that the unity of the Spirit is a gift, it does show us that it is something that we initially have (you cannot keep something you do not already have). This can be seen by the fact that Paul tells us to keep the unity of the Spirit, not work hard to get it. The Greek word for keep is *Tereo,* which means, *to guard from loss or injury by watching out for and keeping an eye upon.* Its root word in the Greek is *Teros,* which means, *a watch.* By stating this, Paul is telling us that the unity of the Spirit is something that we already have and something for which we should look in the midst of the Church. In other words, it is a given that unity is resident in the body of Christ and our responsibility as the church is to keep what the Holy Spirit has brought to us.

The question comes: If we have already received the unity of the Spirit, how, when and by what means did we receive it? It is these three questions that are the crux of what I am seeking to answer in this chapter. I want to show you that the unity of the Spirit is a free gift that has been given to us by God, and we receive this gift through faith in appropriation, as we do the other gifts God has given to us. In order to do this, I will start by showing that the unity of the Spirit is a free gift that we have been given by God.

The Revolutionary Teachings of Paul

Where in scripture does it reveal that the unity of the Spirit is a free gift that God has given to us? This is the question I am seeking to answer. In order to do this, we need to look at a few verses. The first place is Ephesians 2:13-18: *"But now in Christ Jesus, ye who sometimes were afar off are made nigh by the blood of Christ. For He is our peace, who hath made both one, and hath broken down the middle wall of partition between us; having abolished in His flesh the enmity, even the law of commandments contained in ordinances; for to make in himself of twain one new man, so making peace; and that He might reconcile both unto God in one Body by the cross having slain the enmity thereby: And came and preached peace to you which were afar off, and to them that were nigh. For through Him we both have access by one Spirit unto the Father."*

What is Paul seeking to convey to us through these words? Paul is sharing with us the key that will unlock the unity of the Spirit in the Church today. He is sharing with us how genuine unity comes – Christ's redemptive work. In other words, faith appropriation of Christ's redemptive work is the crux of the issue. When we believe in what Christ has done, unity is a natural by-product of this faith. As an example, Paul illustrates how God, through Christ's redemptive work, has brought together both Jews and Gentiles.

The Jewish people had a covenant with God, and through this covenant they had access to God. Gentiles, on the other hand, did not have a covenant with God, and as a result, were separated from God. In other words, an invisible wall was created between the Jewish people and Gentiles by the first covenant. This invisible wall between the Jews and Gentiles promoted hostility. Envy and pride created an impenetrable barrier between us that could not be stripped away through natural means. It literally took an act of God to tear this wall down, bridge the gap and bring unity between the Jewish people and the Gentiles.

What Paul said here was revolutionary at the time he wrote it, and is one of the reasons why he was so hated by his fellow Jews. They were stark raving mad over what Paul said to a degree that we cannot even imagine today. To them, Paul had stripped them of their Jewish identity – the Law of God. They could not understand how Paul could do such a thing. In their minds, Paul was a traitor to his people and, even worse, betraying his own people for the sake of the wicked Gentiles.

We rarely think of this context when we read these passages. We do not understand the real price Paul paid to write these words to us today. By saying what he did, Paul placed all that he had on the line. This was how extreme his words appeared to be to the Jewish people of his day. Paul, because of these very words, was hunted down, beaten and eventually murdered. Paul created problems wherever he went because of what he was saying in these passages of scripture.

A Conflict in Comprehension

Even the other apostles could not completely understand what Paul was saying. James, the brother of the Lord, because of the conflict being created by what Paul was preaching, wanted Gentile believers to come under certain constraints – *"that they abstain from pollutions of idols, and from fornication, and from things strangled, and from blood"* (Acts 15:20).

Paul tolerated this teaching for a time, however, when he wrote his letter to the Corinthians and to Timothy, he said what he really believed:

"As concerning therefore the eating of those things that are offered in sacrifice unto idols, we know that an idol is nothing in the world, and that there is none other God but one" (1 Cor. 8:4).

"For every creature of God is good, and nothing to be refused if it is received with thanksgiving, for it is sanctified by the word of God and by prayer" (1 Tim. 4:4-5).

Paul blatantly fought against any type of bondage to anything that would steal the freedom Christ had purchased for him (and us) at Calvary. Paul did not want

49

to cheapen Christ's work through his own or anyone else's rules, even if it was done for a good reason under the leading of the Holy Spirit.

Peter, in writing of Paul, said this, *"...even as our beloved brother Paul also according to the wisdom given unto him hath written unto you; as also in all his epistles, speaking in them of these things; in which are some things hard to be understood, which they that are unlearned and unstable rest, as they do also the other scriptures, unto their own destruction"* (2 Pet. 3:15-16).

Even Peter did not always understand Paul. However Peter recognized the blessing Paul had been in his life. Without Paul, Peter may very well have caused many other believers to stumble and fall into the very sin Paul identified in Peter, which was the sin of prejudice and national pride. Peter had allowed his cultural beliefs to determine his actions, rather than following the precepts of God. Paul saw this and confronted Peter on it. Paul was unwilling to let anything slide or steal from the redemptive work of Christ. Paul understood what great price Jesus had paid to purchase this freedom and he was unwilling to let anyone take this away, no matter how it looked to those around him.

The Price of Unity

Paul wanted what Christ had paid for so dearly to be manifested in the earth: a Body of believers committed and submitted to the lordship and leading of Christ.

Jesus, in Paul's mind, had paid the ultimate price to unite believers, and Paul was unwilling to allow even the hint of sin to separate us from what Christ had wrought at Calvary. Paul fought with every ounce of his strength to stay unconditionally true to his convictions until the end. In Paul's mind, this is how important Christ's Body was to the plan and purpose of God on planet earth. Paul went so far as to say, *"If any man defile the temple of God, him shall God destroy; for the temple of God is holy, which temple ye are"* (1 Cor. 3:17). Doesn't this sound a bit extreme? Not to Paul. Paul knew just how important Christ's Body was to God. The Father had promised His Son a Body. Paul knew this and recognized that from the beginning this is what the Father had been promising His Son.

The Body of Christ is not an afterthought in the mind of God. No, this had been part of God's covenant plan since the beginning. This promise was sealed by an oath sworn by the Father to the Son and everything that God has and is doing is directly related to this oath. God will offer His Son a Body that is *"without blemish, spot, wrinkle or any such thing"* (Eph. 5:27). Christ is eagerly awaiting the day His Father gives Him the Body for which He has been waiting nearly 2,000 years. There is an earnest expectation in the heart of God, the Father and Son, for this day. We are the key to seeing this day come. We can make God's dream come true as Tommy Tenney says in his book, *The Dream Team.* Understanding and walking in the revelation of the Body of Christ will take nothing less than the miracle working power of God and a revelation of the free gift of the unity of the Spirit.

Christ has paid the price for us to become one. The redemptive work of Christ includes the tearing down of every barrier separating us, as well as the bringing together of every believer in Christ into a Body for Christ. This can be clearly seen in the revelation of the communion as taught by Paul. In speaking of this, Paul says, *"The cup of blessing which we bless, is it not the communion of the blood of Christ? The bread which we break, is it not the communion of the Body of Christ? For we being many are one bread, and one Body: for we are all partakers of that one bread.... For as often as ye eat this bread, and drink this cup, ye do show the Lord's death till He come"* (1 Cor. 10:16-17a; 11:26).

It's His Work, Not Ours

Clearly from these scriptures, one can see that Christ's redemptive work includes provision for the free gift of the unity of the Spirit. Christ has died to make us one. Hence, unity cannot be created by or through anything that we do. We cannot make ourselves become one Body in Christ, and as hard as we may try, what we become will always be different from what God is seeking to create. Genuine unity is born of Christ's redemptive work and can only be brought about by the Holy Spirit's work in the midst of the congregation of believers. Understanding this will help us as we begin to grapple with the questions posed at the beginning of this chapter.

As you may remember, at the beginning we posed three questions, which were: how, when and by what means did we receive the unity of the Spirit? Thus far, we have seen that Christ's redemptive work is the foundation upon which the unity of the Spirit is built. We also know that we cannot create this unity in and of ourselves – it took what Christ did at Calvary to create the ability for us to be in unity. So then, we can begin understanding that the unity of the Spirit is not a product of what we can do, but a result of Christ's redemptive work on our behalf. This means that the unity of the Spirit, like salvation, is and can only be received as a gift freely given to us, not something that we can work to attain.

What I want you to see is that Jesus is the reason we have unity through the Holy Spirit. The unity of the Spirit begins with Christ's redemptive work upon the cross and is a vital part of His redemptive work, just like salvation and healing. This means, just as we receive and walk in salvation and healing by faith, so also can we walk in the free gift of the unity of the Spirit by faith (It takes at least two individuals to walk in this unity of the Spirit by faith). In other words, it is not enough to know about salvation; we must experience it through the appropriation of faith. So also, it is not enough to know about the unity of the Spirit; we must experience it through the appropriation of faith. In this case, the faith that I am talking about appropriating is not only a personal faith as in the case of salvation, but also a corporate faith manifested in the midst of the congregation of the saints. Through an individual and corporate faith imparted by apostolic covering and direction, congregations are able to receive, live and walk in the unity of the Spirit.

Learning how to receive, live and walk in this corporate faith is critical to receiving, living and walking in the free gift of the unity of the Spirit that Christ has purchased for us. The dynamics of appropriating a corporate faith are far different than that of appropriating a personal faith. Because of this, we need to understand what a corporate faith is and how we can walk in it together. To do this, I will explain the principles revealed by Paul in scripture of how we can receive and walk in a corporate faith so that we might become one Body in Christ.

Chapter Five

Becoming One Body in Christ

Now ye are the Body of Christ, and members in particular.

1 Cor. 12:27

C hrist, through his death, has already made us one Body. The Church is the Body of Christ today. And yet, while this is true, it is also true that we are in the process of becoming the Body of Christ. Scholars would describe it this way: The Church today is at this very moment positionally the Body of Christ, however, most believers have not yet learned how to experientially walk in what they are positionally. For this reason, I can say that most of the Church needs to learn how to become the Body of Christ so that we can experientially walk in what we, in fact, are.

Thus far, I have shown that much of the Church has tried to generate its own form of unity rather than walking in the unity of the Spirit given to us by Christ. In truth, most leaders within the Church have not known how or where to begin walking experientially in the unity we have been given positionally. This has resulted in a general frustration in most believers over the lack of unity between churches. Many national leaders have tried to bring unity among local leaders with minimal results. In the end, alliances are created among certain sects of local leaders, which end up bringing further divisions among those not included in these alliances. This is not the model of genuine unity revealed in scripture.

Most of these leaders, who usually mean well, have tried to form Christian unity around the lowest common denominator of beliefs. This approach often legislates the faith of those involved by "majoring on the minors and minoring on the majors." However, this approach, although containing some Biblical precedence, usually causes Pentecostal and Charismatic leaders to take a back seat to those Evangelical leaders involved. The leaders of these meetings, usually Evangelical, often act as moderators seeking to keep the peace by invoking a series of unwritten rules, which prevents the demonstration of any spiritual gifts by those present. Suspicion, fear and control reign in this kind of environment, and those present are kept from walking in their callings in Christ.

Fulfilling Our Destiny

In contrast, Paul in his letter to the Corinthian believers spoke of the Church functioning as the Body of

Christ, where *"as God hath distributed to every man, as the Lord hath called every one, so let him walk. And so ordain I in all churches"* (1 Cor. 7:17). Paul understood that the Body of Christ could only be the Church if believers present were allowed to walk in and fulfill their role in Christ.

This is the crux of what being a member of Christ's Body should bring to individual believers: an atmosphere where every believer is allowed to fulfill his/her role in Christ. The Church can only be the Church in the context of a caring community of believers who are walking in and fulfilling their individual roles in Christ. This is the kind of Church Christ is building, and it is what the Church will fully become before He returns.

Since this is what Christ is seeking in the Church today, how then do we move from what we have been doing into what He is presently doing? The first step as we have seen in previous chapters is for us to receive the free gift of the unity of the Spirit. By receiving this free gift through a corporate faith (I am in the process of writing a more in-depth book on faith entitled *The Tools of Faith.* In this coming book, I will lay a solid foundation for living by and walking in an individual and corporate faith, explaining in detail the principles I am presenting in this book regarding walking in a corporate faith) among members within Christ's Body, we can truly begin walking in the unity revealed in scripture. Hence, understanding and receiving the free gift of the unity of the Spirit is critical to our ability to walk as the Body of Christ. Once we do this, however, there is still the practical matter of keeping the unity that we have received by faith (Eph. 4:3). This is what I will discuss in the remainder of this chapter.

Receiving the free gift of unity is the easy part; keeping it requires hard work. There are things that we must do to keep the unity of the Spirit. In fact, through my studies of the scriptures, I have identified 10 different ways leaders and believers can endeavor to keep the unity Christ has given to us. These things are very practical and down-to-earth ways that leaders and believers can avoid becoming or getting involved in divisive behavior.

Ten Practical Steps to Peace

1. Keep your eyes on Jesus.

2. Abide in God's presence.

3. Listen to the mind and heart of God concerning situations.

4. Don't idolize, envy or be intimidated by those around you.

5. Be honest about what is in your heart without becoming critical.

6. Open the lines of communication for the expression of ideas and thoughts.

7. Allow God to restore your trust in others, especially those in leadership roles.

8. Be willing to change anything you are doing that is affecting the unity of the church.

9. Allow for disagreement when there is a potential for contention (i.e., opinions, doctrines, vision and even what you believe).

10. Major on major things while avoiding contention over minor things at all costs.

1. Keeping our eyes on Jesus

Division usually begins when believers turn their eyes away from the person of Christ to something and/or someone else. Idolization and intimidation have their roots in this kind of spiritual myopia. Distractions like these can do more damage to our spiritual lives than a full frontal assault by the enemy of our soul. The greatest battles we will ever fight will be the ones that seek to turn our eyes from the Person and work of Christ.

This means that keeping our eyes on Jesus is vitally important. Every believer needs to learn how to filter things taking place around him or her through the Person of Christ. Christ has left us an example that is to be emulated today. We have a faithful foundation upon which we can build that will never be shaken. Christ is the Solid Rock upon Whom we are to build our spiritual lives. Building our lives upon Him will prevent us from being shaken when the storms of life do come. And the closer

Christ's coming draws near, the more storms we will have to face in this life. Keeping the unity of the Spirit begins by keeping our eyes on Jesus.

2. Abiding in God's Presence

Genuine unity does not happen by accident, and it does not remain by accident. It requires the supernatural strength of God's abiding presence. Abiding in God's presence is essential to the creation and formation of unity. Genuine unity begins by the Spirit and is sustained by the Spirit. We cannot create unity by ourselves; it is supernatural and is something that can only be created by the Holy Spirit. The Holy Spirit is the one who births and keeps genuine unity in the midst of believers – especially in churches.

Local churches can only walk in real unity to the degree their leadership team allows the Holy Spirit to create, build and integrate the unity of the Spirit into the spiritual foundation of those believers under their care. This is the crux of what leading in the local church is – keeping the unity of the Spirit in the bond of peace in the midst of the congregation. Anyone who disrupts the unity of the Holy Spirit is to be seen as an enemy of the local church. This is a serious matter in the sight of God, and leaders need to take seriously the admonition in scripture to *"mark them which cause divisions and offenses contrary to the doctrine which ye have learned; and avoid them"* (Rom. 16:17). Do not allow anyone or anything to disrupt the unity the Holy Spirit is seeking to bring into the local church by His presence.

3. Hearing From God

God is speaking to us today. We can have an ear to hear what the Holy Spirit is saying regarding specific matters in this life. Wisdom is only a prayer away for those who are able to hear what God is saying. Availing ourselves of God's wisdom and understanding enables us to face situations in this life victoriously every time. We can live above defeat in every area of life, including walking in genuine unity, if we have an ear to hear what the Holy Spirit is telling us to do. This is why listening to what the Holy Spirit is saying is such an important requirement for leadership within the local church.

Every leader within the local church should be able to hear from God clearly on specific matters the church is facing. Leaders who clearly hear from God are vital to the church's ability to keep the unity of the Spirit in the bond of peace. This is why leaders were chosen in the First Century Church according to their ability to hear from God. The same is true today; we need leaders who can clearly hear what the Holy Spirit is saying to the Church.

4. Avoiding Idolatry, Envy and Intimidation

One of the major causes for division in the First Century Church was idolizing, envying or being intimidated by other believers and/or leaders. Many churches struggled with this problem. The Corinthian church struggled with idolizing its leaders. The church in Phillipi had a problem with envying leaders. The Galatian church fell into the subtle trap of being intimidated and manipulated. Almost every church in the New Testament was struggling with glorying in men.

Today, there is little difference among many believers who struggle with glorying in men. The temptation to idolize, envy or be intimidated by those in authority within the church can be overwhelming. The enemy plays upon our fears and desires to get us to give in to this temptation. In fact, this is one of the reasons why so many believers have struggled and suffered within the church. Abusiveness, isolation, manipulation and betrayal fill churches with wounded believers. We must learn how to stop glorying in men.

Overcoming this temptation to glory in men requires diligence, persistence and hard work. What's more, we need to come to the realization of who God is in us and who we are in Him. All of us are created in God's image. No one has the right to lord over, abuse or manipulate us. Leadership in the Body of Christ was never meant to override our own will, unless we are walking in open sin (Matt. 20:25-28; 1 Pet. 5:2-3). Godly leaders know the boundaries of good leadership, and their calling to lead others toward God's will, not push them away from it. God's calling upon us is to be complemented and fulfilled in the context of a caring community of believers who are walking together in one accord. This is what the Church is supposed to be.

5. Learning To Walk Honestly

I think this is one of the toughest areas to walk on a consistent basis for most believers, especially those who are seeking to walk in faith. Sometimes, there is a fine line between presumption and faith. Knowing the difference can make all the difference in the world in our spiritual lives and our ability to walk in genuine unity. Living honestly before the Lord and one another is essential to keeping the unity of the Spirit in the bond of peace.

For this to happen, we need to learn how to be honest with ourselves first. Unless we can be honest with ourselves, we will never be able to walk in honesty with others. Honesty will lead us to the place of transparency, and transparency into the place of intimacy with God and one another. This is why the scriptures admonish us to speak the truth in love (Eph. 4:15) and to have our conversation honest among the Gentiles (1 Pet. 2:12). Honesty protects us from the enemy's lies and preserves us in the midst of a dark world. This is the path to true freedom and genuine unity in Christ.

6. Opening Lines of Communication

The open exchange of ideas and thoughts is foundational to building unity in the Church. Churches that provide a forum for ideas and thoughts to be expressed are able to grow in their kingdom calling and purpose. Sharing in the ideas and thoughts that others bring to table will often precede their own willingness to care in return about what we bring to the table. As we open the doors for the expression of ideas and thoughts, we are also opening the hearts of others to share to the ideas and thoughts we bring. Godly leaders know this and as a results seek to create a place within the church for the free flow of ideas and thoughts.

The Bible talks about this happening in a godly manner within the church – believers coming together and sharing what God is doing in their lives (i.e., testimonies, revelations, rhema words, prayer needs, etc.) When this happens in a godly manner, everyone is built up, stirred up and strengthened in the Lord. As Paul said, *"Let all things be done decently and in order"* (1 Cor. 14:40). *"For God is not the author of confusion, but of peace, as in all the churches of the saints"* (1 Cor. 14:33). I think we need to listen to his admonition, and let all things be done first – meaning, let believers in the midst of the congregation of the saints share and care about what God is doing in one another's life. We need to open the lines of communication in our churches so that unity may be cultivated in our midst.

7. Trust Broken, Trust Restored

One of the hardest things to be restored after it has been broken is trust. Trust is a sacred event that takes place in the heart of a man or woman. When those we love break trust, it can affect every area of our lives. When confidences are betrayed, expectations are unmet or hurtful words are uttered, it can be very easy to slip into a place where we choose never to get hurt to that degree again. Thus, we avoid intimate relationships entirely. I believe this is one of life's hardest lessons to learn.

Every one of us will go through this place of broken trust at some point in our lives, if we haven't already. Some of us have experienced this so many times that we are numb to its effect upon our lives. We don't realize how much damage has been done to us through this area of our own brokenness. When this happens, we need to learn how to run to God, our Rock, as a place of refuge, until our brokenness can be restored. God is in the business of repairing the irreparable and restoring that which cannot be restored. When others do not understand us or what we are enduring, we can rest assured that God does understand, and will answer the deep cries in our hearts. We serve a big God.

8. Becoming Willing To Change

There are things that all of us do that can disrupt the unity of the church. Learning how to identify these problem areas in our own lives and then allowing God to change us is what being part of the Body is all about. None of us is perfect, and all of us need to be willing to change. Change can be a good thing, if it is a change for the better. Positive change requires God's hand moving in our midst and on our behalf, helping us break patterns in our lives that disrupt the flow of His Spirit. Remember, the Holy Spirit is the only One Who can create unity among us.

Our willingness to change our problem areas is a sign of genuine humility. There may even be times where we are right about a matter, but still need to be willing to change for the sake of keeping the unity of the Spirit in the Body of Christ (ie. being doctrinally right, but relationally wrong in attitude or action). Knowing how and when to do this is a sign of Christian maturity. We are to pursue the things that make for peace, not to advocate our own position no matter how right we may be. Being right does not make us part of the Body and cannot make us one, but it can sure divide us. As such, we need to remember the admonition in scripture to *"keep the unity of the Spirit in the bond of peace"* (Eph. 4:3).

9. Agreeing to Disagree

Genuine unity does not necessarily mean that we agree on everything with everyone. In fact, one of the reasons why the Church today is so divided is most of us don't know that there are two different types of unity revealed in scripture. One is called the "unity of the Spirit" and the other is called the "unity of the faith." The first we have been given as a gift; the second we grow into as we learn from the five-fold ministry gifts in the Church. There are differences between the two, which I will not discuss here. Suffice it to say that genuine unity does not begin around individual points of doctrine, but by the Holy Spirit in our midst. It grows as we grow in our understanding of the person of Christ through the fivefold ministry gifts.

Knowing this, we should be more willing to be gracious and supportive of those who don't necessarily think or do what we think or do. There is much diversity in the Church with good reason. We need one another: the good, the bad and even what may appear to be the ugliest parts of the Body of Christ. As Paul said, *"Our comely parts have no need: but God hath tempered the Body together, having given more abundant honor to that part which lacked: That there should be no schism in the Body; but that the members should have the same care one for another"* (1 Cor. 12:24-25).

10. Avoiding Unnecessary Contention

Learning how to major on the majors is a fundamental issue within many churches. One of the main struggles pastors experience is the desire to keep the sheep happy. If pastors or leaders seek to please the sheep, they are run ragged by the sheep. On the other hand, if pastors stop trying to please the sheep, complaining, murmuring and bickering often fill the church. It is a rare pastor or leader who is able to find the balance of pleasing the sheep without being held in bondage to pleasing the sheep.

Finding this place of balance is the crucible of ministry. Those pastors and leaders who are able to find this place of balance are also able to find good success in their churches and/or ministries. Keeping the peace is extremely important in building the church. The church is to be a place of peace. As such, good leaders find ways to avoid unnecessary controversy. There may be times when conflict or controversial issues arise that need to be dealt with, but most of the time these issues are better left in the hands of the Holy Spirit. Knowing how to do this is a sign of a mature leader and someone who has the ability to keep the unity of the Spirit in the bond of peace.

Conclusion

God has called us to peace. We are to be a unified Church under the leadership of the person of the Holy Spirit. The Holy Spirit is not divided from the other members of the Godhead, and we shouldn't be divided from one another. We can use these 10 practical steps to grow in our ability to keep the unity of the Spirit in the bond of peace. My prayer is that God will help us to do exactly this as we move into the third day of the Church through this third reformational move of His Spirit.

As the scripture says, *"Remember ye not the former things, neither consider the things of old. Behold, I will do a new thing; now it shall spring forth..."* (Isa. 43:18-19a).

Other Books Available from Lighthouse Publications

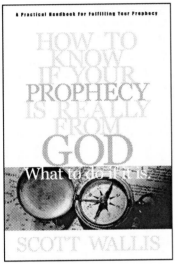

How to Know if Your Prophecy is Really from God

One of the most important books on prophecy available for believers. If you have ever received a prophetic word, then this book will help you discern if that word was from God, and if it was, what to do with it to see if fulfilled.

Author: Scott Wallis
Retail Price: $11.99
ISBN: 1931232415

Plugging into the Spirit of Prophecy

God has designed every believer to walk in the prophetic. You can learn how to flow in the Holy Spirit of prophecy. This exciting book will teach you how to do this and more. You will experience God's awesome power through the prophetic word.

Author: Scott Wallis
Retail Price: $11.99
ISBN: 1931232210

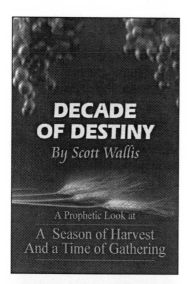

Decade of Destiny

A powerful prophetic word detailing what God is doing in our days. First written in 1991, this timeless book has proven to be an accurate window into the future. Discover what God is saying to His Church today!

Author: Scott Wallis
Retail Price: $11.99
ISBN: 0964221195

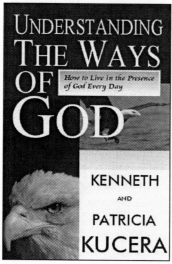

Understanding the Ways of God

You can understand the mysteries behind God's ways. No longer wonder why God does what He does – you can know. As you read this exciting book, you will learn secret after secret of walking in the ways of God. Unlock the potential God has placed inside of you as you learn the ways of God!

Authors: Ken & Pat Kucera
Retail Price: $11.99
ISBN: 0964221152

The Message in the Miracles of Christ

Recently, researchers have discovered that there may be hidden coded messages in the actual text of the Bible. Could it be that the miracles of Jesus also reveal hidden messages of what God is doing in our day? Discover the answer as you read this exciting book!

Author: Donna Carlisle
Retail Price: $14.99
ISBN: 0964221136

Growing in the Spirit

Taking from life examples, Pastor/Prophet Rudy Clark reveals principles of spiritual growth. Through many life lessons, God has taught Reverend Clark the values and virtues that have made him the man he is today. Experience freedom as you learn how to reach your fullest potential.

Author: Rudy Clark
Retail Price: $14.99
ISBN: 0964221160

These and other Christian books from Lighthouse Publications are available at participating local Christian bookstores, Amazon.com & Bn.com.

**To order books directly from Scott Wallis:
Visit www.ScottWallis.org**

<u>Ministry Headquarters</u>
All Nations Worship Center
2028 Larkin Avenue
Elgin, IL 60123
(847) 468-8139

• Additional Resources •

CPSIA information can be obtained at www.ICGtesting.com
Printed in the USA
BVOW021850300912

301706BV00001B/4/A